MY FIRST 30 DUAS
ISLAMIC INVOCATIONS
Taken from the HADITH

This book belongs to :

....
....
....
....

FINESS
EDITION

INTRODUCTION

This little book intended for Muslim children who are not fluent in the Arabic language, it will help them to read, understand and learn about thirty invocations made by the **Prophet Muhammad** ﷺ ,and this through the translation into French, the transcription (phonetic) and the option to scan and listen.

It is possible to define **"Dua"** as an invocation or prayer addressed to Allah. It represents the essence of worship (ibadah). The **Dua** should be the only recourse available to the believer, as it is a conversation with Allah. There are differing views among the faithful about the timing, format and content of this invocation, but there is a broad consensus that it should be performed in a humble, clear, submissive manner and with the certainty that Allah will answer it.

HOW TO MAKE A DUA

1. Present your invocation at the beginning, end or during the prayer (salat);
2. Concentrate so as not to be distracted;
3. Be humble, submissive and trusting;
4. Say your prayer when you feel happy, sad or confused;
5. Don't say a prayer you don't understand;
6. Express yourself concisely, frankly and humbly;
7. Invoke the name of Allah as you begin your Dua ;
8. Repeat the invocations made by the Prophet ;
9. Confess your faults and repent of your sins ;
10. Ask directly for the blessings you wish to receive ;
11. Ask for blessings for others as well ;
12. Avoid negative requests for others or for yourself;
13. You should pray in the firm belief that Allah will answer your invocations,

Invocation of the day (01) دعاء اليوم

اللَّهُمَّ ثَبِّتْنِي وَاجْعَلْنِي هَادِياً مَهْدِيَّاً

«Al-lâhumma thabbitnî waj'alnî hâdiyan mahdiyyan»

«O my God, refine me in the path of righteousness and make me a well-guided man and a guide for others»

Invocation of the day (02) دعاء اليوم

اللَّهُمَّ مُصَرِّفَ القُلُوبِ صَرِّفْ قُلُوبَنَا عَلَى طَاعَتِكَ

« Al-lâhumma muçarrif al- gulûb, çarrif galbî 'alâ tâ'atik»

«O my Lord! You who guide hearts, direct my heart to obey your will»

Invocation of the day (03) دعاء اليوم

اللَّهُمَّ رَبَّنَا آتِنَا فِي الدُّنْيَا حَسَنَةً وَفِي الْآخِرَةِ حَسَنَةً وَقِنَا عَذَابَ النَّارِ

«Al-lâhumma rabbanâ âtinâ fi- d-dunyâ hasanh, wa fi-l-âkhirati hasanah, waginâ 'azhâb an-Nâr»

«O my Lord! Grant us a good portion in this world and a good portion in the Hereafter, and protect us from the punishment of the Fire».

Scan & Listen

Invocation of the day (04) دعاء اليوم

اللَّهُمَّ عَلِّمْنِي الكِتَابَ وَالحِكْمَةِ و فَقِّهْنِي فِي الدِّينِ

«Al-lâhumma 'allimnî al-kitâb wal-hikma, wa faggihnî fi-d-dîn»

«O my Lord, teach me the Qur'an and grant me wisdom, and deepen my knowledge of religion».

Scan & Listen

Invocation of the day (05) دعاء اليوم

اللَّهُمَّ إِنِي أَسْأَلُكَ الهُدَى، وَالتُّقَى، وَالعفَافَ، والغنَى

«Al-lâhumma innî 'as'luka al- hudâ wat-tugâ, wa'afâf wal- ghinâ»

«O my Lord! Direct me to the path of righteousness and grant me piety, preserve my chastity, and grant me good fortune»

Invocation of the day (06) دعاء اليوم

اللَّهُمَّ اغْفِرْ لِي جِدِّي وَهَزْلِي وَخَطَئِي وَعَمْدِي وَكُلُّ ذَلِكَ عِنْدِي

«Al-lâhumma 'aghfir lî hazalî wa jiddî, wa khata'î wa 'amdî, wa kulu zhâlika 'indî

«O my Lord! Forgive me for the misdeeds I have committed in jest or in firmness, by unintentional or deliberate act. For all this, alas, applies to me».

Invocation of the day (07) دعاء اليوم

اللَّهُمَّ إِنِّي أَعُوذُ بِكَ مِنَ الْكَسَلِ وَالْهَرَمِ وَالْمَأْثَمِ وَالْمَغْرَمِ

«Al-lâhumma innî 'a'ûzhu bika min al-kasal wal-haram, wal- ma'tham wal-maghram»

«My Lord! Preserve me from laziness and decadence. Protect me from any temptation leading to an illicit act and preserve me from the burden of debts».

Invocation of the day (08) دعاء اليوم

اللَّهُمَّ اغْفِرْ لي وارْحَمْني واجعلني مع الرَّفيقِ الأعلى

«Al-lâhumma 'aghfir lî warhamnî, waj'alnî ma'a ar-rafîg al- 'alâ »

«O my Lord! Grant me Your forgiveness and show me mercy. And make me one of the chosen ones»

Scan & Listen

Invocation of the day (09) دعاء اليوم

اللَّهُمَّ إِنِّي أَعُوذُ بِكَ مِنْ شَرِّ مَا عَمِلْتُ، وَمِنْ شَرِّ مَا لَمْ أَعْمَلْ

«Al-lâhumma innî 'a'ûzhu bika min charri mâ 'amiltu wa min charri mâ lam 'a'mal»

«O my God, I seek Your protection against every evil that I have done and against every misdeed that I would commit»

Scan & Listen

Invocation of the day (10) دعاء اليوم

اللَّهُمَّ إِنِّي أَعُوذُ بِكَ مِنْ جَهْدِ الْبَلَاءِ، وَدَرَكِ الشَّقَاءِ، وَسُوءِ الْقَضَاءِ، وَشَمَاتَةِ الْأَعْدَاءِ

«Al-lâhumma innî 'a'ûzhu bika min jahdi-l-balâ', wa daraki-ch-chagâ', wa sû'i-l-gadhâ', wa chamâtati-l-'a'dâ'»

«O my Lord, I seek Your protection against the suffering of trial, against the hardest misery, against evil spells and against the malignant joy of enemies»

Scan & Listen

Invocation of the day (11) دعاء اليوم

اللَّهُمَّ أَنْتَ الْمَلِكُ لاَ إِلَهَ إِلاَّ أَنْتَ، أَنْتَ رَبِّي وَأَنَا عَبْدُكَ ظَلَمْتُ نَفْسِي وَاعْتَرَفْتُ بِذَنْبِي فَاغْفِرْ لِي ذُنُوبِي جَمِيعًا إِنَّهُ لاَ يَغْفِرُ الذُّنُوبَ إِلاَّ أَنْتَ

«Al-lâhumma 'anta-l-Malik, lâ ilâha illâ 'anta, 'anta rabbî wa'anâ 'abduk, zalamtu nafsî a'taraftu bizhanbî faghfir lî zhunûbî jamî'an, innahû lâ yaghfiru-zh- zhunûba illâ 'ant»

«O Allah, You are the Absolute Sovereign. There is no god but You. You are my Lord, and I am Your servant-adorator. I have wronged myself, and I confess my faults to you. So forgive me all my sins, because no one blots out sins except You»

Invocation of the day (12) دعاء اليوم

لاَ إِلَهَ إِلاَّ اللَّهُ وَحْدَهُ أَعَزَّ جُنْدَهُ وَنَصَرَ عَبْدَهُ وَغَلَبَ الأَحْزَابَ وَحْدَهُ فَلاَ شَيْءَ بَعْدَهُ

«Lâ illâha illa-l-Lâh wahdahu, 'a'azza jundah, wa naçara 'abdah, wa ghalaba al-ahzâba wahdah, falâ chay'a ba'dah»

«There is no god but Allah, the One God, Who has brought glory to His army, Who has granted victory to His servant, and Who alone has routed the army of adversaries. He is the Last (and nothing succeeds Him)».

Scan & Listen

Invocation of the day (13) دعاء اليوم

اللَّهُمَّ آتِ نَفْسِي تَقْوَاهَا، وَزَكِّهَا أَنْتَ خَيْرُ مَن زَكَّاهَا، أَنْتَ وَلِيُّهَا وَمَوْلَاهَا

«Al-lâhumma âtî nafsî tagwâhâ, wa zakkihâ 'anta khayro man zakkâhâ, 'anta waliyyuhâ wa mawlâhâ»

«O my Lord, fill my soul with piety and purify it, for You are the Best who can do it. You are indeed its Master and Protector».

Invocation of the day (14) دعاء اليوم

اللَّهُمَّ إِنِّي أَعُوذُ بِكَ مِنْ زَوَالِ نِعْمَتِكَ، وَتَحَوُّلِ عَافِيَتِكَ، وَفُجَاءَةِ نِقْمَتِكَ، وَجَمِيعِ سَخَطِكَ

«Al-lâhumma innî 'a'ûzhu bika min zawâli ni'matik, wa tahawwuli 'âfiyatik, wa fujâ'ti nigmatik, wajamîT sakhatik»

«O my Lord, I seek Your protection against the disappearance of the blessings You have bestowed upon me, against ill health, against any sudden misfortune and against any form of Your anger».

Scan & Listen

Invocation of the day (15) دعاء اليوم

اللَّهُمَّ اجْعَلْنِي يَوْمَ الْقِيَامَةِ فَوْقَ كَثِيرٍ مِنْ خَلْقِكَ مِنَ النَّاسِ، وَأَدْخِلْنِي يَوْمَ الْقِيَامَةِ مُدْخَلاً كَرِيمًا

«Al-lâhumma 'aj'alnî yawm al-giyâmati fawga kathîrin min khalgika min an-nâs, wa 'adkhilinî yawm al-giyâmati mudkhalan karîman»

«O my God! Grant me a higher rank than many of Your human creatures, and let me enter an honorable abode (Paradise)»

Scan & Listen

Invocation of the day (16) دعاء اليوم

اللَّهُمَّ إِنِّي أَعُوذُ بِكَ مِنْ عِلْمٍ لاَ يَنْفَعُ وَمِنْ قَلْبٍ لاَ يَخْشَعُ وَمِنْ نَفْسٍ لاَ تَشْبَعُ وَمِنْ دعوة لا يستجاب لها

«Al-lâhumma innî 'a'uzhu bika min 'ilmin lâ yanfa', wa min galbin lâ yakhcha4, wa min nafsin lâ tachba', wa min da'watin lâ yustajâbu lahâ»

«O my Lord, I seek Your protection against all useless knowledge, against a hard and insubordinate heart, against a soul full of greed and lust, and against an invocation that is not answered by You».

Scan & Listen

Invocation of the day (17) دعاء اليوم

لَا إِلَهَ إِلَّا اللهُ الْعَظِيمُ الْحَلِيمُ، لَا إِلَهَ إِلَّا اللهُ رَبُّ الْعَرْشِ الْعَظِيمِ، لَا إِلَهَ إِلَّا اللهُ رَبُّ السَّمَوَاتِ وَرَبُّ الْأَرْضِ وَرَبُّ الْعَرْشِ الْكَرِيمِ

«Lâ illâha illa-l-Lâh al-'azîm al-halîm, lâ illâha illa-l-Lâh rabbu- l-'arch al-'azîm, Lâ illâha illa-l- Lâh rabbu-s-Samâwâti wa rabbu-1- 'ardh wa rabbu-l-'arch al-karîm»

«There is no god but Allah, the Most Great, the Most Clement. There is no God but Allah, the Lord of the Throne. There is no god but Allah, the Lord of the heavens and the earth, the Lord of the Sublime Throne».

Invocation of the day (18) دعاء اليوم

اللَّهُمَّ لا مانِعَ لِما أعطيتَ ، ولا مُعطِيَ لِما منعتَ ، ولا رادَّ لِما قضيتَ ، ولا ينفعُ ذا الجَدِّ منك الجَدُّ

«Al-Lâhumma lâ mâni'a limâ 'a'tayt wa lâ mu'tî limâ mana't wa lâ yanfa'u zha al-jaddi minka al-jadd»

«O Allah! no one can withhold what Thou givest, or give what Thou withholdest, and riches cannot avail a wealthy person with Thee»

Scan & Listen

Invocation of the day (19) دعاء اليوم

اللَّهُمَّ إِنِّي أَعُوذُ بِعِزَّتِكَ، الَّذِي لَا إِلَهَ إِلَّا أَنْتَ، الَّذِي لَا يَمُوتُ، وَالْجِنُّ وَالْإِنْسُ يَمُوتُونَ

«Al-lâhumma innî 'a'ûzhu bi'izzatika-l-lazhî lâ ilâha illâ 'anta-l-lazhî lâ yamûtu wal-Jinnu wal-Insu yamûtûn»

«O my Lord! I take refuge in Your power. There is no god but Thee, the Immortal, while the Jinn as well as men are all mortal ».

Scan & Listen

Invocation of the day (20) دعاء اليوم

اللَّهُمَّ اغْفِرْ لِي ذَنْبِي كُلَّهُ، دِقَّهُ وَجِلَّهُ، وَأَوَّلَهُ وَآخِرَهُ، وَعَلَانِيَتَهُ وَسِرَّهُ

«Al-lâhumma 'aghfir lî zhanbî kullahu, diggah wajillah, wa 'awwalah wa âkhirah, wa'alâniyatah wa sirrah»

«O my God, erase from me all my misdeeds, whether they be small or great, first or last, apparent or hidden».

Scan & Listen

Invocation of the day (21) دعاء اليوم

اللهُمَّ أَعُوذُ بِرِضَاكَ مِنْ سَخَطِكَ، وَبِمُعَافَاتِكَ مِنْ عُقُوبَتِكَ، وَأَعُوذُ بِكَ مِنْكَ لَا أُحْصِي ثَنَاءً عَلَيْكَ أَنْتَ كَمَا أَثْنَيْتَ عَلَى نَفْسِكَ

«Al-Lâhumma 'a'ûzhu biridhâka min sakhatika, wa bimu'âfâtik min 'ugûbatik, wa aûzhu bika mink, lâ 'uhçî thanâ'an 'alaya, 'anta kamâ 'athnayta 'alâ nafsik»

«O my Lord, protect me by Your pleasure from Your wrath, and protect me by Your forgiveness from Your punishment. I take refuge in You against You. I praise Thee without end, Thou Who hast pleased Thyself»

Invocation of the day (22) دعاء اليوم

اللَّهُمَّ إِنِّي ظَلَمْتُ نَفْسِي ظُلْمًا كَثِيرًا، وَلا يَغْفِرُ الذُّنُوبَ إِلاَّ أَنْتَ، فَاغْفِرْ لِي مَغْفِرَةً مِنْ عِنْدِكَ، وَارْحَمْنِي، إِنَّكَ أَنْتَ الْغَفُورُ الرَّحِيمُ

«Al-lâhumma innî zalamtu nafsî zulman kathîran, wa lâ yaghfiru-z-zunûba illâ 'anta, faghfir lî maghfiratan min 'indik warhamnî, innaka 'anta-l-ghafûru-r-rahîm»

«O my God, I have done much wrong to myself, and no one forgives sins but You. Therefore, grant me forgiveness from You, and have mercy on me. You are indeed the Great Forgiver, the All-Merciful»

Invocation of the day (23) دعاء اليوم

اللَّهُمَّ إِنِّي أَعُوذُ بِكَ مِن فِتْنَةِ النَّارِ وعَذابِ النَّارِ، وفِتْنَةِ القَبْرِ وعَذابِ القَبْرِ، وشَرِّ فِتْنَةِ الغِنَى وشَرِّ فِتْنَةِ الفَقْرِ

«Al-lâhumma innî 'a'ûzhu bika min fitnati-n-Nâr wa 'azhâbi-n-Nâr, wa fitnati-l-gabr wa 'azhâbi-l-gabr, wa charri fitnati-l-fagr»

«O my God, protect me from the trial of the Fire and its punishment. Preserve me from the trial of the grave and its torment. I seek Your protection, O Lord, against the trial of wealth (as a temptation) and against the trial of poverty»

Invocation of the day (24) دعاء اليوم

رَبَّنَا لَكَ الْحَمْدُ، مِلْءَ السَّمَاوَاتِ وَالأَرْضِ، وَمِلْءَ مَا شِئْتَ مِنْ شَيْءٍ بَعْدُ، أَهْلَ الثَّنَاءِ وَالْمَجْدِ، أَحَقُّ مَا قَالَ الْعَبْدُ، وَكُلُّنَا لَكَ عَبْدٌ،

«Al-Lâhumma rabbanâ laka-1- hamd, mil'a-s-Samâwâti wal- 'ardh, wa mil'a mâ chi'ta min chay'in ba'd, 'ahlu-th-thanâ'i wal-majd, 'ahaggu mâ gâl al-'abd, wa kullunâ laka 'abd»

«O my Lord, the praises are Thine, filling the heavens and the earth and filling everything else Thou wilt. Thou art worthy of the best praise and all glory, for these are the best true words that a servant has ever spoken, and we are all Thy servants».

Scan & Listen

Invocation of the day (25) دعاء اليوم

اللَّهُمَّ إِنِّي أَعُوذُ بِكَ مِنَ الْعَجْزِ وَالْكَسَلِ، وَالْجُبْنِ وَالْهَرَمِ وَالْبُخْلِ، وَأَعُوذُ بِكَ مِنْ عَذَابِ الْقَبْرِ، وَمِنْ فِتْنَةِ الْمَحْيَا اَلْمَمَاتِ

«Al-lâhumma innî 'a'ûzhu bika min al-'ajz wal-kasal, wal-jubn wal-bukhl. Wa'a'ûzhu bika min azhâb al-gabr, wa 'a'ûzhu bika min fitnat al-mahyâ wal-mamât»

«My God, I take refuge in You against helplessness and laziness, against cowardice and greed. I seek Your protection, O Lord, against the torment of the grave, against the trial (fascination) of life and against the trial of death».

Invocation of the day (26) دعاء اليوم

اللَّهُمَّ اغْفِرْ لِي مَا قَدَّمْتُ وَمَا أَخَّرْتُ، وَمَا أَسْرَرْتُ وَمَا أَعْلَنْتُ، أَنْتَ المُقَدِّمُ وَأَنْتَ المُؤَخِّرُ، وَأَنْتَ عَلَى كُلِّ شَيْءٍ قَدِيرٌ

«Al-lâhumma 'aghfîr lî mâgaddamtu wamâ 'akhkhart, wa mâ 'asrartu wa mâ 'a'lant, 'anta al-mugaddim wa 'anta al- mu'akhkhir, wa 'anta 'alâ kulli chay'in gadîr»

«My God! Forgive me my past sins and my future sins, forgive me what I disclose and what I hide inside. It is You Who raises people in rank and Who lowers them. You are Omnipotent! ».

Scan & Listen

Invocation of the day (27) دعاء اليوم

اللَّهُمَّ اغْسِلْ قَلْبِي بِماءِ الثَّلْجِ وَالبَرَدِ، وَنَقِّ قَلْبِي مِنَ الخَطايا كَما نَقَّيْتَ الثَّوْبَ الأبْيَضَ مِنَ الدَّنَسِ، وَباعِدْ بَيْنِي وَبَيْنَ خَطايايَ كَما باعَدْتَ بَيْنَ المَشْرِقِ وَالمَغْرِبِ

«Al-lâhumma aghsil galbî bimâ'i-th-thalj wal-barad, wanaggî galbî min al-khatâyâ kamâ naggayta-th-thawb al-abyadh min ad-danas, wa bâ'id baynî wa bayna khatâyây kamâ bâ'adta bayna-1- machrig wal-maghrib».

«My Lord, wash my heart with the water of snow and hail, and purify it from misdeeds as You purified the white garment from all impurity. My God, remove me from my sins as You removed the East from the West».

Invocation of the day (28) دعاء اليوم

اللَّهُمَّ اجْعَلْ فِي قَلْبِي نُورًا، وَفِي بَصَرِي نُورًا، وَفِي سَمْعِي نُورًا، وَعَنْ يَمِينِي نُورًا، وَعَنْ يَسَارِي نُورًا، وَفَوْقِي نُورًا، وَتَحْتِي نُورًا، وَأَمَامِي نُورًا، وَخَلْفِي نُورًا، وَاجْعَلْ لِي نُورًا

«Al-Lâhumma aj'al fî galbî nûran, wa fî baçarî nûran, wa fî sama'î nûran, wa 'an yamînî nûran, wa 'an yasârî nûran, wa fawgî nûran, wa tahtî nûran, wa 'amâmî nûran, wa khalfî nûran wa 'azzim lî nûran»

«Oh my Lord! Put a light in my heart, a light in my sight (my eyes), a light in my hearing (my ears), a light on my right hand, a light on my left hand, a light above me and a light below me, a light in front and a light behind me, and let it be a good light».

Invocation of the day (29) دعاء اليوم

اللَّهُمَّ أَصْلِحْ لِي دِينِي الذي هو عِصْمَةُ أَمْرِي، وَأَصْلِحْ لِي دُنْيَايَ الَّتِي فِيهَا معاشِي، وَأَصْلِحْ لِي آخِرَتِي الَّتِي فِيهَا معادِي، وَاجْعَلِ الحَيَاةَ زِيَادَةً لِي في كُلِّ خَيْرٍ، وَاجْعَلِ المَوْتَ رَاحَةً لِي مِن كُلِّ شَرٍّ

«Al-lâhumma 'açlih lî dînî al-lazhî huwa 'içmatu 'amrî, waçlih lî dunyây al-latî fîhâ ma'âchî, wa açlih lî âkhiratî al-latî fîhâ ma'âdî, waj'al al-hayâta ziyâdatan lî fi kulli khayr, waj'al al-mawta râhatan lî min kulli char».

«O my Lord, consolidate my belief which is the safeguard of my soul, and improve my life in this world where I get my sustenance. O my Lord, give me a beautiful share in the Hereafter where I will be brought back, and make my life full of blessings and death a salvation for me from all misfortune».

Scan & Listen

Invocation of the day (30) دعاء اليوم

اللَّهُمَّ أَنْتَ رَبِّي لاَ إِلَهَ إِلَّا أَنْتَ، خَلَقْتَنِي وَأَنَا عَبْدُكَ، وَأَنَا عَلَى عَهْدِكَ وَوَعْدِكَ مَا اسْتَطَعْتُ، أَعُوذُ بِكَ مِنْ شَرِّ مَا صَنَعْتُ، أَبُوءُ لَكَ بِنِعْمَتِكَ عَلَيَّ، وَأَبُوءُ لَكَ بِذَنْبِي فَاغْفِرْ لِي، إِنَّهُ لاَ يَغْفِرُ الذُّنُوبَ إِلَّا أَنْتَ

«Al-lâhumma 'anta rabbî lâ ilâha illâ 'anta, khalagtanî wa 'anâ 'abduk, wa 'anâ 'alâ 'ahdika wa wa'dik mastata'tu, 'a'ûzhu bika min charri mâ çana'tu 'abû' laka bini'matika 'alayyâ, wa 'abû' laka bizhanbî faghfir lî, fa'innahu la yaghfiru-zh-zhunûba illâ 'ant»

«O Allah! You are my Lord. There is no god but Thee. You have created me and I am Your servant-worshipper. I submit to my commitment to You and to Your promise as much as possible. I seek refuge in You against the evil that I have committed. I am grateful for the blessings You have bestowed upon me and I confess my sins to You. Forgive me then, for no one blots out sins but You».

THE END

May Allah bless you and put the blessing on you

Made in the USA
Middletown, DE
25 March 2023